Guided Reading Notes

Purple Band
Oxford Level 8

Habitat

Contents

Introduction	2
Escape of the Giant Chicken (Fiction)	6
Attack of the Centipede (Fiction)	13
The Monster of the Deep (Fiction)	20
Dinosaur Safari (Non-fiction)	27
Dangerous Creatures (Non-fiction)	34

Introduction

Why is guided reading important?

Guided reading plays an important role in your whole-school provision for reading, providing opportunities for children to progress and develop the key competencies they need to become confident and skilled independent readers. Working with small groups of children, with texts closely matched to the readers' needs, guided reading is the perfect vehicle for delivering focused teaching from Reception/PI right through to Year 6/P7. The teacher-pupil interaction also provides a valuable assessment opportunity, helping you identify exactly what each child can and can't do. Through guided reading children also encounter a world of exciting, whole books – building a community of readers who read for pleasure.

About *Project X Origins*

Project X Origins is a comprehensive, whole-school guided reading programme designed to help you teach the wide range of skills essential to ensure children progress as readers and to help nurture a love of reading.

Ensuring the key skills are covered

Project X Origins incorporates all of the key skills children need to develop to become successful and enthusiastic readers:

> **Word reading:** phonically regular and common exception words are introduced systematically in the early levels with phonic opportunities provided throughout the notes. As children progress, they are encouraged to use their decoding skills whenever they encounter new or unfamiliar words, and also to recognize how this impacts on different spelling rules.

> **Comprehension:** understanding what has been read is central to being an effective and engaged reader but comprehension is not something that comes automatically so specific strategies have been built into the notes to ensure children develop comprehension skills they can use over a range of texts:

- Previewing
- Predicting
- Activating and building prior knowledge
- Questioning
- Recalling
- Visualizing and other sensory responses
- Deducing, inferring and drawing conclusions
- Determining importance
- Synthesizing
- Empathizing
- Summarizing
- Personal response, including adopting a critical response

> **Reading fluency:** fluency occurs as children develop automatic word recognition, reading with pace and expression. Strategies to help achieve this, including meaningful opportunities for oral reading, re-reading and re-listening are provided throughout.

> **Vocabulary:** introducing new vocabulary within a meaningful context is an important element in extending children's vocabulary range, developing their reading fluency and comprehension. Each thematic cluster provides opportunities for revisiting and reinforcing vocabulary over a range of books and contexts.

> **Grammar, punctuation and spelling:** learning about language in the context of a text, rather than through a series of discrete exercises, can help make grammar, punctuation and spelling relevant and helps children make the link between grammar, punctuation and clarity of meaning, thus supporting their development as writers. Opportunities to support an in-depth look at language are provided for every book from Year 1/P2 to Year 6/P7.

> **Spoken language:** talk is crucial to learning and developing their comprehension so children are given plenty of opportunities to: discuss and debate their ideas with others; justify their opinions; ask and answer questions; explore and hypothesise; summarise, describe and explain; and listen and respond to the ideas of others.

Assessment and progression in reading

Project X Origins includes a rigorous assessment spine drawn from the *Oxford Reading Criterion Scale* to ensure that you know exactly what each child can do and what they need to focus on next in order to make progress. This assessment framework, combined with the careful levelling of the Oxford Levels, will help you select the right book with the right level of challenge for each of your guided reading groups and to assess, track and monitor each child's progress.

Step 1

On a termly basis, use the *Oxford Reading Criterion Scale* (which can be found in the relevant *Project X Origins Teaching Handbook*) to assess each child's reading. The scale will tell you the Oxford Level a child is comfortable reading at, and the areas a child needs to develop. You can also use this assessment to form your guided reading groups.

Step 2

Plan your guided reading sessions by selecting books at the appropriate Oxford Level that focus on the relevant learning needs of the group. You will find charts showing the learning objectives and assessment points for every *Project X Origins* book in the relevant *Project X Origins Teaching Handbook*. Depending on your assessment, you might choose a book at the level the children are comfortable at or one from the next level up, to offer some stretch.

Step 3

Use the assessment points within the Guided Reading Notes to support on-going assessment of children's reading progress. The Progress Tracking Charts in the relevant *Project X Origins Teaching Handbook* can be used to record this if you wish. Regularly re-assess each child's progress combining your on-going informal assessments and the termly assessment using the *Oxford Reading Criterion Scale*. Use this information to re-organize guided reading groups and teaching plans in response to children's varying degrees of progress.

Getting started: using the Guided Reading Notes

> **At a glance**
> *Project X Origins* Guided Reading Notes offer detailed guidance to help deliver effective and engaging guided reading sessions, and are designed to be used flexibly to ensure you get the most out of each book. For notes containing multiple sessions, you may choose to focus on each of these sessions or focus on one session and have the children read the rest of the book independently.

Curricular correlation and assessment
At the beginning of every set of notes there are correlation charts for all UK curricula, ensuring that across the clusters the main curricular objectives are covered. In addition, an overview of assessment points for each book is provided – these points are also signposted throughout the notes.

Key information
Before the first session, an overview of the book and the resources you will need (such as additional photocopy masters) is provided.

Teaching sequence
Each guided reading session follows the same teaching sequence:

- **Before reading**: children explore the context of each book to support their understanding and help them engage with the text. They are encouraged to discuss, recall, respond, predict and speculate about the book. Opportunities to focus on word reading and/or vocabulary are also introduced at this point.
- **During reading**: children are given a section of the book to read with specific questions in mind.
- **After reading**: children reflect on and discuss what they have read. They are encouraged to delve deeper, exploring their understanding of the text, developing their vocabulary, grammar, punctuation, spelling and fluency where appropriate.
- **Follow-up**: opportunities for children to extend their learning outside the session are provided, including writing and cross-curricular activities.

Throughout the sessions, the key strategies that children are developing are clearly identified.

Escape of the Giant Chicken
BY JAN BURCHETT AND SARA VOGLER

Curricular correlation
English National Curriculum

Spoken language	Use spoken language to develop understanding through speculating, hypothesising, imagining and exploring ideas
Word reading	Read words containing common suffixes
Comprehension	Check that the text makes sense to them as they read and correct inaccurate reading
	Discuss the sequence of events in books and how items of information are related
	Recognise simple recurring literary language in stories

Phonics and vocabulary

GPCs	/er/ eagerly, early, first, worked /or/ boring, bought, squawked
Decodable 2 and 3 syllable words	visitors, gobbled
Common exception words	eyes, where, can't
Challenge and context words	yolk, strutted, brainwave, escape, flapped, perched, scrambled, chicken, tiptoed, café, tempt

Developing grammar, punctuation and spelling

Grammar and Punctuation	Co-ordination	and, but
Spelling	Adding the endings -ing and -ed to words ending in -e with a consonant before it	gobbled, tiptoed, boring, coming, exciting, scrambled, waved

Reading assessment points (Oxford Reading Criterion Scale: Assessment Standard 3)

1. Can the children identify when reading does not make sense and self-correct in order for the text to make sense? (READ)
3. Can the children apply phonic skills and knowledge to recognize an increasing number of complex words? (READ)
7. Can the children make predictions about a text using a range of clues? (D)
9. Can the children provide simple explanations about events or information? (D)
18. Can the children summarise a story, giving the main points clearly in sequence? (R)
21. Can the children talk about how different words and phrases affect meaning? (E)

Scottish Curriculum for Excellence

Listening and talking	I can communicate clearly when engaging with others within and beyond my place of learning, using selected resources as required LIT 1-10a
Reading	I can use my knowledge of sight vocabulary, phonics, context clues, punctuation and grammar to read with understanding and expression ENG 1-12a
	I am learning to select and use strategies and resources before I read, and as I read, to help make the meaning of texts clear LIT 1-13a
	I can share my thoughts about structure, characters and/or setting, recognise the writer's message and relate it to my own experiences, and comment on the effective choice of words and other features ENG 1-19a

Foundation Phase Framework in Wales

Oracy	Adopt a specific role, using appropriate language in structured situations (Speaking)
	Contribute to discussion, keeping a focus on the topic and taking turns to speak (Collaboration and discussion)
Reading	Apply the following reading strategies with increasing frequency to a range of familiar and unfamiliar texts: phonic strategies; recognition of HFW; context clues, e.g. prior knowledge; graphic and syntactic clues; self-correction, including re-reading and reading ahead (Reading strategies)
	Show understanding and express opinions about language, information and events in texts (Response and analysis)
	Recall and retell narratives and information from texts with some details (Comprehension)

Northern Ireland Curriculum

Talking and Listening	Take turns at talking and listening in group and paired activities
Reading	Use a range of strategies to identify unfamiliar word
	Begin to use evidence from text to support their views
	Recognise and notice how words are constructed and spelt

Escape of the Giant Chicken

About this book

Max, Cat, Ant and Tiger are on a day out at the city farm. But when Ant's watch goes wrong, they soon find they have a huge problem on their hands – an escaped giant chicken!

You will need

- *Egg-stra words* Photocopy Master, *Teaching Handbook* for Year 2/P3
- *Egg-cellent jokes* Photocopy Master, *Teaching Handbook* for Year 2/P3

Before reading

- Talk to the children about farms. Have any of them visited a farm? What sort of animals would they expect to find on a farm? **(activating prior knowledge)**
- Look at page 2 and discuss the characters in the book. Which character is new to the series? **(previewing)**
- Read pages 3–6 to the children, modelling expression and pace. What do the children think about the story so far? What do they think the other children might say to Tiger? **(personal response, predicting)**
- Ask the children what to do if they encounter a difficult word, modelling with an example from the book.
- Discuss with the children what to do if they struggle to understand the meaning of a word or a sentence, e.g. rereading the word or sentence again.

Assessment point

Can the children make predictions about a text using a range of clues? (ORCS Standard 3, 7)

Phonic opportunity

- Write the word *early* on the board. Tell the children that there are many words in this story which have the /**er**/ phoneme in them. Refer them to words such as *first* and *worked*. Ask them to think of other words with the /er/ sound.
- Now look at words with the /**or**/ phoneme: *boring*, *bought*, *squawked*.
- You may also wish to point out some of the common exception words or practise decoding some of the challenge and context words in this book.

Assessment point

Can the children apply phonic skills and knowledge to recognize an increasing number of complex words? (ORCS Standard 3, 3)

During reading

- Ask the children to read from page 7 to the end of the book.
- Ask the children to look out for verbs ending -ing and -ed as they read.

Assessment point
Can the children identify when reading does not make sense and self-correct in order for the text to make sense? (ORCS Standard 3, 1)

After reading

Returning to the text

- What caused Shelly to get bigger? **(recall)**
- How did the children get Shelly to come down from the café roof? **(recall)**
- Ask the children to create a character profile about Shelly the chicken. How did the characters' knowledge of Shelly's personality help them to get her off the roof? **(determining importance)**
- Ask one child to take the role of Shelly the chicken. How did she feel when she began to grow? Explore Shelly's feelings. **(empathizing)**

Assessment point
Can the children provide simple explanations about events or information? (ORCS Standard 3, 9)

Shelly began to scratch at the café roof. "She's trying to dig a hole!" gasped Cat. "No she's not," said Ant, as Shelly sat down. "She's laying an egg!"

Yuck!

Shelly clucked proudly. She stood up and a giant egg rolled out from underneath her. It rolled down the roof and ... SPLAT! It hit the ground.
"We've been scrambled!" groaned Tiger.

Developing comprehension

- Using information from the story, ask the children to create a map of the farm and the park, plotting the places where the key events took place. **(visualizing)**
- Next to the places on the map, ask the children to write the key events of the story. **(summarizing)**

Assessment point
Can the children summarise a story, giving the main points clearly in sequence?
(ORCS Standard 3, 18)

Developing vocabulary

- Invite the children to read the jokes on page 24 to each other. Do the children know any other jokes about animals? Allow them to tell the jokes with appropriate expression and gestures.
- Look at the word *egg-citing* on page 23. Why do the children think the authors have used this word? Can they make up other funny words beginning with the word *egg*? e.g. *egg-stra, egg-stravagant, egg-sercize*. The children could write these on the *Egg-stra words* Photocopy Master.

Assessment point
Can the children talk about how different words and phrases affect meaning?
(ORCS Standard 3, 21)

> ### Developing grammar, punctuation and spelling

- Look at page 20 and ask the children to identify the sentence that uses the word *but*. Discuss that this is an example of co-ordination. The word *but* joins groups of words (clauses) that are of the same importance in the sentence. Do the same with the sentence on page 21 using the word *and*. Challenge the children to identify another example of this in the book.
- Look at the words the children have found ending *-ing* or *-ed*. Discuss how when these suffixes are added to root words that end in an 'e', that the 'e' needs to be removed before adding the suffix, e.g. *gobble* - *gobbled*. Explain that this rule can also be applied to adding *-er*, *-est* and *-y* to words that end in an 'e'.

Follow-up

Writing activities

- Ask the children to write a character profile of Shelly the chicken, giving details about her appearance, personality, her likes and dislikes. **(short writing task)**
- Together, think of other animals and consider what might happen if they grew beyond their normal size. What might the consequences be? Ask the children to write a story about a giant animal. **(longer writing task)**
- Ask the children to write speech bubbles for two or more characters on page 8, to show what they are thinking or feeling. **(short writing task)**

Other literacy activities

- Ask the children to practise reading the jokes on the *Egg-cellent jokes* Photocopy Master to each other. If they want to, encourage them to make up their own jokes. **(spoken language)**

Cross-curricular activities

- Ask the children to draw a key for the farm/park map. Explain that they will be continuing to expand the map after reading the next story. **(Geography)**
- Create problem-solving activities relating to eggs. **(Maths)**
- Create stop-frame animations using toy farm animals and modelling clay. **(Computing)**

Attack of the Centipede
BY JAN BURCHETT AND SARA VOGLER

Curricular correlation
English National Curriculum

Spoken language	Articulate and justify answers, arguments and opinions
Word reading	Read further common exception words, noting unusual correspondence between spelling and sound
Comprehension	Make inferences on the basis of what is being said and done
	Draw on what they already know or on background information and vocabulary provided by the teacher
	Listen to, discuss and express views about a range of stories at a level beyond that at which they can read independently

Phonics and vocabulary

GPCs	/s/ snakes, city, centipede, voice, pressed /er/ towered, worms, turn, firmly
Decodable 2 and 3 syllable words	snorted, escaped, compost, hatch, dial
Common exception words	something, through, head
Challenge and context words	wormery, recycling, centipede, crocodile, wriggling, Australian, escaped, carnivore

Developing grammar, punctuation and spelling

Grammar and Punctuation	Apostrophes to mark where letters are missing in spelling	I've, isn't, It's, You're, He's, What's, I'm, Let's, Don't
Spelling	The /ur/ sound spelt 'or' after 'w'	worm, wormery, working

Reading assessment points (Oxford Reading Criterion Scale: Assessment Standard 3)

2. Can the children read aloud, taking into account . ? ! ? (READ)
3. Can the children apply phonic skills and knowledge to recognize an increasing number of complex words? (READ)
6. Can the children locate some specific information e.g. key events, characters' names or key information in a non-fiction text? (R)
7. Can the children make predictions about a text using a range of clues? (D)
8. Can the children compare similarities and differences between texts in terms of characters, settings and themes? (D/E)
14. Can the children read words with contractions (e.g. I'm, I'll, we'll, he's) and understand that the apostrophe represents the omitted letter(s)? (READ)
20. Having read a text, can the children find the answers to questions, both written and oral? (R)

Scottish Curriculum for Excellence

Listening and talking	I regularly select and listen to or watch texts which I enjoy and find interesting, and I can explain why I prefer certain sources LIT 1-01a
Reading	I can use my knowledge of sight vocabulary, phonics, context clues, punctuation and grammar to read with understanding and expression ENG 1-12a
	I can share my thoughts about structure, characters and/or setting, recognise the writer's message and relate it to my own experiences, and comment on the effective choice of words and other features ENG 1-19a
	I am learning to select and use strategies and resources before I read, and as I read, to help make the meaning of texts clear LIT 1-13a
	I regularly select and read, listen to or watch texts which I enjoy and find interesting, and I can explain why I prefer certain texts and authors LIT 1-11a

Foundation Phase Framework in Wales

Oracy	Express opinions, giving reasons, and provide appropriate answers to questions (Speaking)
	Contribute to discussion, keeping a focus on the topic and taking turns to speak (Collaboration and discussion)
Reading	Apply the following reading strategies with increasing frequency to a range of familiar and unfamiliar texts: phonic strategies; recognition of HFW; context clues, e.g. prior knowledge; graphic and syntactic clues; self-correction, including re-reading and reading ahead (Reading strategies)
	Read a range of suitable texts with increasing accuracy and fluency (Reading strategies)
	Draw upon relevant personal experience and prior knowledge to support understanding of texts (Comprehension)
	Express views about information and details in a text (Response and analysis)

Northern Ireland Curriculum

Talking and Listening	Express thoughts, feelings and opinions in response to personal experiences, imaginary situations, literature, media and curricular topics and activities
Reading	Use a range of strategies to identify unfamiliar words
	Express opinions and give reasons based on what they have read

About this book
Tiger shrinks to micro-size to explore a wormery. But there are more than just worms to think about. A giant centipede is on the loose. Will Tiger escape?

You will need
- *Character profile* Photocopy Master, *Teaching Handbook for Year 2/P3*
- *Centipede fact file* Photocopy Master, *Teaching Handbook for Year 2/P3*

> Before reading

- If you have read the previous book in the cluster, *Escape of the Giant Chicken*, ask the children what they remembered about the farm. **(activating prior knowledge)**
- Look at the front cover. What do the children predict might happen in this story? Which of the characters do they think might be involved? Why? **(predicting)**
- Look at page 2 to find out which new characters are in this story. **(previewing)**
- Take a picture walk through the book. Draw the children's attention to some of the more unusual vocabulary to enable them to read the story fluently. **(introducing new vocabulary)**

Assessment point
Can the children make predictions about a text using a range of clues? (ORCS Standard 3, 7)

> *Phonic opportunity*

- Draw attention to all of the words with the /s/ phoneme: *snakes, city, centipede, voice, pressed*. Ask the children to identify the phoneme /s/ in the words. Support the children to say each phoneme and then blend the phonemes to read the word. Ask them to think of other words with the /s/ sound.
- Now look at words with the /er/ phoneme: *towered, worms, turn, firmly*.
- You may also wish to point out some of the common exception words or practise decoding some of the challenge and context words in this book.

Assessment point
Can the children apply phonic skills and knowledge to recognize an increasing number of complex words? (ORCS Standard 3, 3)

- Read pages 3 and 4 aloud to the children, modelling how to build up expression with your voice. Remind them to take note of punctuation, such as exclamation marks and question marks, when reading.
- Ask the children what to do if they encounter a difficult word, modelling with an example from the book.
- Discuss with the children what to do if they struggle to understand the meaning of a word or a sentence, e.g. rereading the word or sentence again.

> **Assessment point**
> Can the children read aloud, taking into account . ? ! ?
> (ORCS Standard 3, 2)

> During reading

- Ask the children to read from page 5 to the end of the book.
- As they read, ask them to focus on the new things they discover about the city farm.

> **Assessment point**
> Can the children locate some specific information?
> (ORCS Standard 3, 6)

> After reading

Returning to the text

- Why couldn't Ant shrink to micro-size? **(recall)**
- Do they think Tiger was right to go into the wormery for Ant? What does this tell us about Tiger's character? **(deducing, inferring and drawing conclusions)**
- How does this story compare with the other story about the city farm? What features of the farm were the same? What was new or different? **(recall, synthesizing, summarizing)**

> **Assessment point**
> Can the children compare similarities and differences between text in terms of characters, settings and themes?
> (ORCS Standard 3, 8)

Developing comprehension

- Ask the children to return to the map of the farm if they previously drew one. Is there anything they want to add to the map or change, based on their further understanding of the setting? Do they need to add any other items to their key? **(synthesizing, visualizing)**
- Talk about the things Tiger says and does in the story. What do these show us about his personality? **(recall, empathizing, personal response)**
- Using the *Character profile* Photocopy Master, ask the children to write information about Tiger to start building up a character profile of him. **(deducing, inferring and drawing conclusions)**
- Ask the children to write down one question relating to centipedes, or looking after worms in a wormery, that they would like to find out about. **(questioning)**
- Allow them, in turn, to read their question out to the group. Similar questions could be combined and then the children could research the answers outside the session.

Assessment point
Having read a text, can the children find the answers to questions both written and oral? (ORCS Standard 3, 20)

Developing vocabulary

- Focus on alliteration, e.g. *wiggly worms wriggling*. Ask the children to act out being worms and then write alliterative phrases. What other alliterative animals could they be? e.g. *slithery snakes sliding, careful cats creeping*. Encourage the children to act out their animal actions. You could take photographs of the actions and ask the children to add their alliterative phrases to the display.

→ **Developing grammar, punctuation and spelling**

- Draw attention to the use of apostrophes to show where letters are missed out of a word (contractions), e.g. *it's*, *let's*. Explain that the apostrophe replaces a letter, so in *it's*, the second 'i' is replaced by the apostrophe. Look through the book with the children and identify where else apostrophes have been used in contractions.

- Write the words *worm* and *working* on the board and ask the children for the sound that they can hear in each. Discuss how the /ur/ sound is sometimes spelt with an 'or'. Can they think of any other examples?

Assessment point

Can the children read words with contractions (e.g. I'm, I'll, we'll, he's) and understand that the apostrophe represents the omitted letter(s)? (ORCS Standard 3, 14)

❯ Follow-up

Writing activities

- Create a poster to advertise a day trip to the city farm. Ask the children to think about why people should visit it and what they can do there. **(short writing task)**
- The children could write a story about meeting a giant animal and include alliterative phrases to interest the reader. **(longer writing task)**
- Use the *Centipede fact file* Photocopy Master to find out and write facts about centipedes. **(short writing task)**

Other literacy activities

- In groups, ask the children to discuss whether they would have gone into the wormery for a friend. Why or why not? **(spoken language, discussion)**

Cross-curricular activities

- Set up a wormery in the classroom to enable the children to become familiar with the concept. **(Science)**
- Talk about city farms with the children. Why have they become so important for children? You could link this with an author focus on Michael Morpurgo and his 'Farms for City Children'. **(PSHE)**
- The children might like to research the answers to their questions about centipedes, and/or looking after a wormery, in books and on the Internet. **(Science, Computing)**

The Monster of the Deep
BY SHOO RAYNER

Curricular correlation
English National Curriculum

Spoken language	Ask relevant questions to extend their understanding and build vocabulary and knowledge
Word reading	Read accurately words of two or more syllables
Comprehension	Draw on what they already know or on background information and vocabulary provided by the teacher
	Make inferences on the basis of what is being said and done
	Predict what might happen on the basis of what has been read so far

Phonics and vocabulary

GPCs	/ow/ growled, out, found /j/ joking, giant, gigantic, orange
Decodable 2 and 3 syllable words	plastic, heron, pretend
Common exception words	water, friends
Challenge and context words	monster, water boatman, island, gigantic, plastic, maze, enormous, poisoning, wrappers, heron, pretend

Developing grammar, punctuation and spelling

Grammar and Punctuation	Expanded noun phrases for description and specification	the monster of the deep, shiny, orange sweet wrappers, needle-sharp beak, the monster of the sky
Spelling	The /l/ sound spelt -le at the end of words	middle, paddle, needle, pile, able, bottle

Reading assessment points (Oxford Reading Criterion Scale: Assessment Standard 3)

3. Can the children apply phonic skills and knowledge to recognize an increasing number of complex words? (READ)
7. Can the children make predictions about a text using a range of clues? (D)
15. Can the children read aloud with intonation, taking into account a wider range of punctuation (. ? ! ,)? (READ)
21. Can the children talk about how different words and phrases affect meaning? (E)
23. Are the children beginning to read between the lines, using clues from text and pictures, to discuss thoughts, feelings and actions? (D)
24. Can the children confidently relate texts to their own experiences? (D)

Scottish Curriculum for Excellence

Listening and talking	When I engage with others, I know when and how to listen, when to talk, how much to say, when to ask questions and how to respond with respect LIT 1-02a
Reading	I can use my knowledge of sight vocabulary, phonics, context clues, punctuation and grammar to read with understanding and expression ENG 1-12a
	I can share my thoughts about structure, characters and/or setting, recognise the writer's message and relate it to my own experiences, and comment on the effective choice of words and other features ENG 1-19a
	To show my understanding, I can respond to different kinds of questions and other close reading tasks and I am learning to create some questions of my own ENG 1-17a

Foundation Phase Framework in Wales

Oracy	Express opinions, giving reasons, and provide appropriate answers to questions (Speaking)
	Show understanding of what they have heard by asking relevant questions to find out specific information (Listening)
Reading	Apply the following reading strategies with increasing frequency to a range of familiar and unfamiliar texts: phonic strategies; recognition of HFW; context clues, e.g. prior knowledge; graphic and syntactic clues; self-correction, including re-reading and reading ahead (Reading strategies)
	Read aloud with attention to punctuation, including full stops, question, exclamation and speech marks, varying intonation, voice and pace (Reading strategies)
	Express views about information and details in a text (Response and analysis)

Northern Ireland Curriculum

Talking and Listening	Devise and ask questions to find information in social situations and across the curriculum
Reading	Use a range of strategies to identify unfamiliar words
	Begin to locate, select and use texts for specific purposes
	Express opinions and give reasons based on what they have read

The Monster of the Deep

About this book

In this adventure, the four friends discover that the local pond is covered in litter and many of the fish and pond life are missing. They decide to clean up the pond, but soon discover that there is more to the mystery of the missing fish than meets the eye.

You will need

- *Pond life* Photocopy Master, *Teaching Handbook* for Year 2/P3
- *Save our pond!* Photocopy Master, *Teaching Handbook* for Year 2/P3
- A large picture of a pond (optional)

Before reading

- Look at the cover of the book and talk about the title. What might this story be about? What could 'The Monster of the Deep' look like? **(predicting)**
- Talk to the children about ponds they have visited. Is there a pond at school? Do they have one at home? Display a large picture of a pond, either on a display board or interactive whiteboard, if you have one. Ask the children to draw and label any pond animals or plants that they know about. **(activating prior knowledge)**
- Take a picture walk through the story, but stop before you reach the picture of the heron to avoid spoiling the story for the children. Can the children use the pictures to predict the story? Do they really think there is a 'Monster of the Deep'? **(previewing, predicting)**

Phonic opportunity

- Write the word *giant* on the board. Tell the children that there are many words in this story which have the /j/ phoneme in them. Refer them to words such as *joking* and *orange*. Ask them to think of other words with the /j/ sound.
- Now look at words with the /ow/ phoneme: *growled*, *out*, *found*.
- You may also wish to point out some of the common exception words or practise decoding some of the challenge and context words in this book.

Assessment point

Can the children apply phonic skills and knowledge to recognize an increasing number of complex words? (ORCS Standard 3, 3)

- Ask the children what to do if they encounter a difficult word, modelling with an example from the book.
- Discuss with the children what to do if they struggle to understand the meaning of a word or a sentence, e.g. rereading the word or sentence again.

> **During reading**

- Ask the children to read pages 2–10 only.
- As they read, ask them to think about how they would feel if a local pond looked like the one in the story.

Assessment point

Can the children confidently relate texts to their own experiences, including story settings and incidents? (ORCS Standard 3, 24)

> **After reading**

Returning to the text

- What did the characters use to help them get the litter from the edge of the pond? **(recall)**
- How do the children think Max, Cat, Ant and Tiger will clear the pond safely? **(deducing, inferring and drawing conclusions)**
- Are the children any closer to guessing what the 'Monster of the Deep' might be? **(predicting)**

Assessment point

Can the children make predictions about a text using a range of clues (e.g. experience of books written by the same author, experience of books already read on a similar theme, book title, cover and blurb)? (ORCS Standard 3, 7)

Developing comprehension

- Before the children discover that it is the heron that is taking the fish, ask them to work in groups to generate questions and hypothesize about what is happening to the pond life. **(questioning)**
- Ask the children to draw pictures of what they think the 'Monster of the Deep' might look like. Encourage them to think of the features it might need to have, based on their knowledge of the story. **(visualizing)**
- Why do the children think the author keeps getting Tiger to say things like *"Watch out for the Monster of the Deep?"* How does this fit in with his character? **(deducing, inferring and drawing conclusions)**

Assessment point
Are the children beginning to read between the lines, using clues from text and pictures, to discuss thoughts, feelings and actions?
(ORCS Standard 3, 23)

Developing vocabulary

- Create a large display with the picture of the pond if you have one, or use the one on the *Pond life* Photocopy Master.
- As the children research and find out more about a pond habitat – ideally by visiting one – ask them to draw pictures of the pond animals or plants and put them on the display with labels and captions.
- The the children could give short presentations about the habitat, using the pictures as prompts.

Developing grammar, punctuation and spelling

- Write the word *beak* on the board and ask the children to explain what picture they have in their heads. Now write *needle-sharp beak* on the board and ask them how their image has changed. Discuss how the expanded noun phrase adds detail and makes the information more specific for the reader. Challenge the children to look through the book and identify other examples of expanded noun phrases that add specific details.

- Write the words *middle* and *bottle* on the board and ask the children for the sound that they can hear in each. Discuss how the /l/ sound is often spelt with an 'le' at the end of a word. Can they think of any other examples?

Assessment point
Can the children talk about how different words and phrases affect meaning?
(ORCS Standard 3, 21)

Developing fluency

- Ask the children to read pages 11–22, encouraging them to use their voices to build suspense. When they feel confident, ask them to perform their reading to a partner or group. **(performance)**

Assessment point
Can the children read aloud with intonation, taking into account a wider range of punctuation (. ? ! ,)?
(ORCS Standard 3, 15)

> Follow-up

Writing activities

- Design a poster advising people not to throw litter in the pond. **(short writing task)**
- Use the *Save our pond!* Photocopy Master to plan a letter to persuade people to keep the pond clean. **(longer writing task)**
- Write facts about different animal species found in a pond. The children might like to create a PowerPoint slide presentation on their chosen animal. **(short writing task)**

Other literacy activities

- Ask the children to record oral sentences to persuade people to take care of the pond. These short recordings could be added to the children's Powerpoint presentations. **(spoken language)**

Cross-curricular activities

- Investigate the relationships between predators and prey in a pond. **(Science)**
- Explore pond habitats and the conditions they need to stay healthy. **(Science)**
- Encourage the children to get involved in a local community project to help keep an area clean. **(PSHE)**
- Use junk and recycled materials to make pond animals and birds. **(Art and Design, DT)**

Dinosaur Safari
BY CLAIRE LLEWELLYN

Curricular correlation
English National Curriculum

Spoken language	Consider and evaluate different viewpoints, attending to and building on the contributions of others
Word reading	Read accurately by blending the sounds in words that contain the graphemes taught so far, especially recognising alternative sounds for graphemes
Comprehension	Read non-fiction books that are structured in different ways
	Discuss the sequence of events in books and how items of information are related
	Make inferences on the basis of what is being said and done

Phonics and vocabulary

GPCs	/or/ horns, dinosaur, warm, more, jaws /oo/ food, through
Decodable 2 and 3 syllable words	predator, fossils, safari
Common exception words	know, through, because
Challenge and context words	brachiosaurus, triceratops, tyrannosaurus, maiasaura, pteranodons, hang-glider, flippers, dinosaur, binoculars, fierce, dangerous, prehistoric, creature, height, surface

Developing grammar, punctuation and spelling

Grammar and Punctuation	How the grammatical patterns in a sentence indicate its function as a statement, question, exclamation or command	What did the earth look like then? (question) Dive to pages 14-17 … (command) Grab some binoculars and let's go on safari! (exclamation) We know which animals lived in the past by looking at fossils. (statement)
Spelling	The /u/ sound spelt 'o'	some, covered, front, among, other, come

Reading assessment points (Oxford Reading Criterion Scale: Assessment Standard 3)

2. Can the children read aloud, taking into account ? ! ? (READ)
3. Can the children apply phonic skills and knowledge to recognize an increasing number of complex words? (READ)
20. Having read a text can the children find the answers to questions, both written and oral? (R)
25. Are the children beginning to talk about the features of certain non-fiction texts? (A)
26. Can the children demonstrate how to use information books? (R/A)

Scottish Curriculum for Excellence

Listening and talking	I can show my understanding of what I listen to or watch by responding to and asking different kinds of questions LIT 1-07a
Reading	I can use my knowledge of sight vocabulary, phonics, context clues, punctuation and grammar to read with understanding and expression ENG 1-12a
	Using what I know about the features of different types of texts, I can find, select, sort and use information for a specific purpose LIT-14a
	I can share my thoughts about structure, characters and/or setting, recognise the writer's message and relate it to my own experiences, and comment on the effective choice of words and other features ENG 1-19a

Foundation Phase Framework in Wales

Oracy	Contribute to discussion, keeping a focus on the topic and taking turns to speak (Collaboration)
Reading	Apply the following reading strategies with increasing frequency to a range of familiar and unfamiliar texts: phonic strategies; recognition of HFW; context clues, e.g. prior knowledge; graphic and syntactic clues; self-correction, including re-reading and reading ahead (Reading strategies)
	Identify and use text features, e.g. titles, headings and pictures, to locate and understand specific information (Reading strategies)
	Show understanding and express opinions about language, information and events in texts (Response and analysis)
	Express views about information and details in a text (Response and analysis)

Northern Ireland Curriculum

Talking and Listening	Think about what they say and how they say it
Reading	Use a range of strategies to identify unfamiliar words
	Explore and begin to understand how texts are structured in a range of genres
	Express opinions and give reasons based on what they have read

About this book

This book explores the different habitats in which dinosaurs lived a hundred million years ago.

You will need

- *Dinosaur jigsaw* Photocopy Master, *Teaching Handbook* for Year 2/P3
- *Prehistoric habitats* Photocopy Master, *Teaching Handbook* for Year 2/P3
- A3 paper, enough for each pair of children

Before reading

- Look through the section headings on the contents page. What do the children know about the different habitats? What different animals do they think might live in each habitat? **(activating prior knowledge, predicting)**
- Take a picture walk through the book. Which dinosaurs do the children recognize? Practise saying some of the names of the dinosaurs, using the pronunciation key in the dinosaur fact boxes to help them. **(word reading, previewing)**
- Read pages 2 and 3. Can the children imagine what the earth might have looked like 100 million years ago? **(visualizing)**

Phonic opportunity

- Give the children the *Dinosaur jigsaw* Photocopy Master and ask them to cut out the jigsaw pieces and put them together to form three different dinosaurs. This activity could make a good assessment of the children's current phonic knowledge.
- Draw attention to all of the words with the /**or**/ phoneme: *horns, dinosaur, warm, more, jaws*. Ask children to identify the phoneme /or/ in the words. Support the children to say each phoneme and then blend the phonemes to read the word. Ask them to think of other words with the /or/ sound.
- Now look at words with the /**oo**/ phoneme: *food, through*.
- You may also wish to point out some of the common exception words or practise decoding some of the challenge and context words in this book.

Dinosaur Safari

- Ask the children to find the words written in bold. Can they tell you what they mean? Look up the words in the Glossary on page 24 and compare these with the children's definitions. **(introducing new vocabulary)**
- Ask the children what to do if they encounter a difficult word, modelling with an example from the book.
- Discuss with the children what to do if they struggle to understand the meaning of a word or a sentence, e.g. rereading the word or sentence again.

> **Assessment point**
> Can the children apply phonic skills and knowledge to recognize an increasing number of complex words? (ORCS Standard 3, 3)

During reading
- Ask the children to read from page 4 to the end of the book.
- As they read, ask them to focus on how the text has been set out on the page. How does this help the reader?

After reading
Returning to the text
- Why did brachiosaurus have long necks? **(recall)**
- Why did triceratops live in forests? **(recall)**
- Why was a swamp a good habitat for the tyrannosaurus? **(deducing, inferring and drawing conclusions)**
- Using the dinosaur fact boxes, ask the children to decide which dinosaur was the biggest. **(synthesizing)**
- What do they think were the advantages of being a tyrannosaurus? **(deducing, inferring and drawing conclusions, determining importance)**

> **Assessment point**
> Having read a text, can the children find the answers to questions, both written and oral? (ORCS Standard 3, 20)

Developing comprehension

- Give out the *Prehistoric habitats* Photocopy Master, asking the children to decide in which habitat each of the four prehistoric creatures lived. **(recall, synthesizing)**

- Look at the non-fiction features in each dinosaur section of the book. Ask the children to identify which ones are the same across the whole book, e.g. the yellow dinosaur fact boxes. How does this layout help the reader? **(determining importance, adopting a critical stance)**

- How do the labels and captions help to support the text? **(determining importance, personal response)**

Assessment point

Can the children demonstrate how to use information books? (ORCS Standard 3, 26)

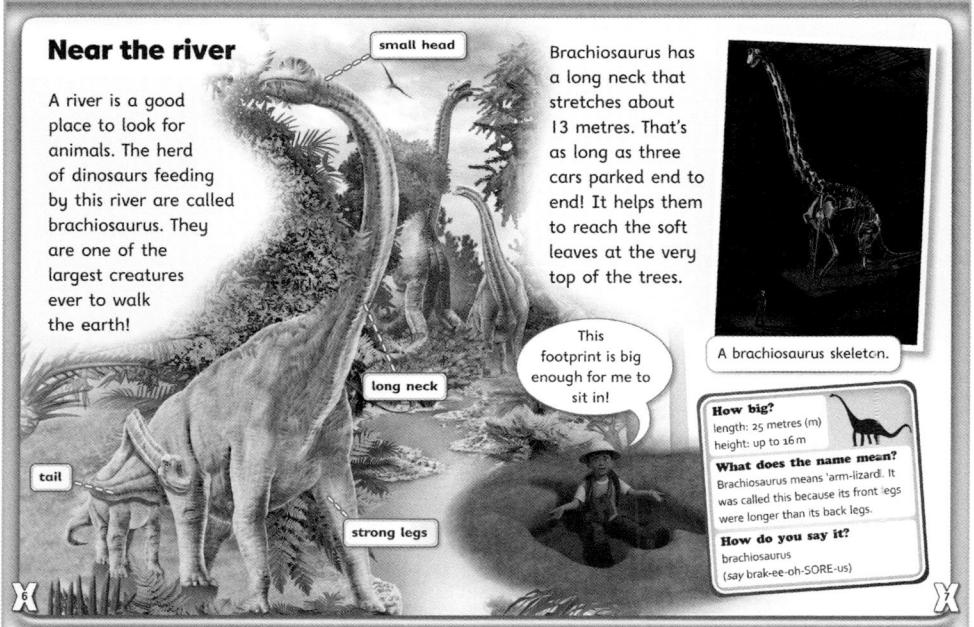

Developing vocabulary

- Working in groups, with each group choosing one of the habitats they have read about, ask the children to brainstorm words and phrases used to describe the habitat. Display these words in the classroom and add to them when children discover appropriate words.

Developing grammar, punctuation and spelling

- Turn to pages 2 and 3 and ask the children to identify a statement, exclamation, question and command on these pages. Discuss the punctuation that is used for each and the words that help indicate the sentence type. Give each child a double-page spread of their own to look at and identify the types of sentence on each. Give time for each child to explain their conclusions to the rest of the group.

- Write the words *some* and *mother* on the board and ask children for the sound that they can hear in each. Discuss how the /u/ sound is sometimes spelt with an 'o'. Can they think of any other examples?

Assessment point

Can the children read aloud, taking into account . ? ! ?
(ORCS Standard 3, 2)

Developing fluency

- Organise the children into small groups. Display a folded A3 sheet of paper and ask the children to discuss how information on another dinosaur might best be laid out to make it interesting and helpful for the reader. Ask each child to contribute their view and to consider each other' alternatives.
- Agree on a layout and ask the children, in pairs, to choose another dinosaur and plan and sketch sections of their own.
- Ask each pair to present their ideas back to the group.

Assessment point
Are the children beginning to talk about the features of certain non-fiction texts? (ORCS Standard 3, 25)

Follow-up

Writing activities

- Ask the children to write further speech bubbles giving other information that Ant might say about each dinosaur. **(short writing task)**
- Allow the children time to research and write the information about their dinosaur. These could be put together to make a class dinosaur book. **(longer writing task)**
- Write a plan for an adventure story for the Project X characters as if the characters have gone back in time and met the dinosaurs. **(short writing task)**

Other literacy activities

- Use small world materials to explore dinosaur adventures, where the children go back in time to discover dinosaurs roaming the land. **(spoken language)**

Cross-curricular activities

- Investigate the different habitats described in the book and map where they can be found around the world. **(Geography)**
- Make model dinosaurs and then create habitats for them. **(DT)**
- Make stop-frame animations using small world dinosaurs. **(Computing)**

Dangerous Creatures
BY ALISON BLANK

Curricular correlation
English National Curriculum

Spoken language	Articulate and justify answers, arguments and opinions
Word reading	Read most words quickly and accurately without overt sounding and blending
Comprehension	Read non-fiction books that are structured in different ways
	Draw on what they already know or on background information and vocabulary provided by the teacher
	Discuss their favourite words and phrases

Phonics and vocabulary

GPCs	/oa/ ocean, mosquito, soaked, home, grow
Decodable 2 and 3 syllable words	wetlands, lizards, humans, hunted
Common exception words	different, found, where, home, every, more, other, many
Challenge and context words	equator, savannah, paralyse, venom, tentacles, blubber, aggressive, mosquitoes, ferocious, poisonous

Developing grammar, punctuation and spelling

Grammar and Punctuation	Commas to separate items in a list	Older crocodiles feast on turtles, frogs, lizards, wild pigs and deer.
Spelling	The /s/ sound spelt 'c' before 'e' and 'i'	place, twice, once, ocean, surface, cells, ice, central, substance, certain, pieces, ferocious, pacific, scientists

Reading assessment points (Oxford Reading Criterion Scale: Assessment Standard 3)

3.	Can the children apply phonic skills and knowledge to recognize an increasing number of complex words? (READ)
6.	Can the children locate some specific information e.g. key events, characters' names etc. or key information on a non-fiction page? (R)
17.	Can the children explain the meaning of 'WOW' words in context (e.g. despair, marvel) including words with common prefixes and suffixes (e.g. undecided, forgetful)? (D)
24.	Can the children confidently relate texts to their own experiences? (D)

Scottish Curriculum for Excellence

Listening and talking	I am exploring how pace, gesture, expression, emphasis and choice of words are used to engage others, and I can use what I learn ENG I-03a
Reading	I can use my knowledge of sight vocabulary, phonics, context clues, punctuation and grammar to read with understanding and expression ENG I-12a
	Using what I know about the features of different types of texts, I can find, select, sort and use information for a specific purpose LIT-I4a
	I can share my thoughts about structure, characters and/or setting, recognise the writer's message and relate it to my own experiences, and comment on the effective choice of words and other features ENG I-19a

Foundation Phase Framework in Wales

Oracy	Adopt a specific role, using appropriate language in structured situations (Speaking)
Reading	Apply the following reading strategies with increasing frequency to a range of familiar and unfamiliar texts: phonic strategies; recognition of HFW; context clues, e.g. prior knowledge; graphic and syntactic clues; self-correction, including re-reading and reading ahead (Reading strategies)
	Use the different features of texts to make meaning, e.g. pictures, charts and layout (Reading strategies)
	Show understanding and express opinions about language, information and events in texts (Response and analysis)
	Express views about information and details in a text (Response and analysis)

Northern Ireland Curriculum

Talking and Listening	Take turns at talking and listening in group and paired activities
Reading	Use a range of strategies to identify unfamiliar words
	Recognise some forms and features of texts
	Explore and begin to understand how texts are structured in a range of genres
	Express opinions and give reasons based on what they have read
	Talk with the teacher about ways in which language is written down, identifying phrases, words, patterns or letters and other features of written language

Dangerous Creatures

About this book
This book explores the habitats of dangerous creatures around the world and why they are dangerous.

You will need
- *Snap!* Photocopy Master, *Teaching Handbook* for Year 2/P3. NB. These cards will need to be enlarged and cut out before the session.
- *Wanted!* Photocopy Master, *Teaching Handbook* for Year 2/P3.

▶ Before reading

- Take a picture walk through the book. Talk to the children about the different animals and habitats. On a large piece of paper ask the children to work as a group to write down the different animals that they recognize. Next to each animal ask them to begin to write or draw anything they know about the animal and its habitat. They can then revisit this concept map as they read through the book. **(activating prior knowledge)**

- Hand out the animal cards from the *Snap!* Photocopy Master and let the children play *Snap!* or *Pairs* to help them become familiar with the different vocabulary. Introduce the habitat cards, this time asking the children to match the habitat to the animal. **(introducing new vocabulary)**

  Assessment point
  Can the children locate some specific information e.g. key events, characters' names etc. or key information on a non-fiction page? (ORCS Standard 3, 6)

- Ask the children if they have ever seen a nature programme, e.g. one narrated by David Attenborough. Talk about how the narrator uses their voice to sound knowledgeable about the subject. Model reading the introduction on pages 2 and 3 to the children. Ask the children to read the same pages aloud, encouraging them to sound like an expert on a nature programme. **(engaging readers)**

  Assessment point
  Can the children confidently relate texts to their own experiences? (ORCS Standard 3, 24)

Phonic opportunity

- Draw attention to all of the words with the /**oa**/ phoneme: *ocean, mosquito, soaked, home, grow*. Ask children to identify the phoneme /oa/ in the words. Support children to say each phoneme and then blend the phonemes to read the word. Ask children to think of other words with the /oa/ sound.
- List some key phonemes that the children have been reviewing or find difficult, e.g. /ae/, /qu/, /oi/. Ask them to carry out a detective hunt to spot words in the book with the different phonemes.
- You may also wish to point out some of the common exception words or practise decoding some of the challenge and context words in this book.

Assessment point
Can the children apply phonic skills and knowledge to recognize an increasing number of complex words?
(ORCS Standard 3, 3)

- Ask the children what to do if they encounter a difficult word, modelling with an example from the book.
- Discuss with the children what to do if they struggle to understand the meaning of a word or a sentence, e.g. rereading the word or sentence again.

During reading

- Ask the children to read from page 4 to the end of the book.
- As they read, ask them to notice the different parts of the world where the different animals live.

After reading

Returning to the text

- What do polar bears have that help them to swim? **(recall)**
- Why do the children think that the ice melting in the Arctic means there will be less food for the polar bears? **(deducing, inferring and drawing conclusions)**
- Ask the children which animal in the book they would least like to meet and why. **(personal response)**

Developing comprehension

- Ask the children to try to plot on a world map where all the different animals live. **(building prior knowledge, synthesizing)**
- Return to the children's concept maps and ask them to add any new information they have discovered. **(summarizing)**
- Ask the children to review their concept map and the world map. What have they learned about animals and their habitats? **(synthesizing)**

Developing vocabulary

- Discuss the theme of danger in the book. Ask the children to look for words and phrases the author has used to bring this theme across and discuss their impact, e.g. *attack, aggressive* (p.5), *ferocious, strong* (p.7), *poisonous, paralyse* (p.11), *squeeze their prey to death* (p.15), *venomous* (p.17), *swallow their prey whole* (p.19).

Assessment point
Can the children explain the meaning of 'WOW' words in context, (e.g. despair, marvel) including words with common prefixes and suffixes (e.g. undecided, forgetful)? (ORCS Standard 3, 17)

Developing grammar, punctuation and spelling

- Write the sentence *Older crocodiles feast on turtles, frogs, lizards, wild pigs and deer* (p.18) on the board. Can the children identify the punctuation mark that appears three times here? Discuss that it is a comma and it can be used to separate things in a list.

- Write the words *place* and *scientists* on the board and ask the children for the sound that they can hear in each. Discuss how the /s/ sound is sometimes spelt with an 'c' before the letters 'e' and 'i'. Can they think of any other examples?

Follow-up

Writing activities

- Use the *Wanted!* Photocopy Master as a poster writing frame to warn people about one of the dangerous creatures they have read about. **(short writing task)**
- Ask the children to create some information pages for a different animal in the same style as those in the book. **(longer writing task)**
- The children could invent a dangerous monster and label its dangerous features. **(short writing task)**

Other literacy activities

- Ask the children to rehearse reading different chapters of the book. When they feel confident, record them reading them, as if they were narrating a nature programme.
(spoken language, performance)

Cross-curricular activities

- Investigate other animals that live in the same habitats as those in the book. **(Science, Geography)**
- Design a habitat for a chosen animal, reminding the children that they need to take into account the specific needs of the animal. **(DT)**
- Use photographs and images to create a collage of one of the dangerous animals. **(Art and Design)**